Bette Davis

A Bette Davis

Biography

Katy Holborn

Table of Contents

Legacy: Larger Than Life

No One Better Than Bette

Introduction

One of the greatest pop songs of all time, is about one of the greatest actresses of all time.

Bette Davis Eyes was written by Jackie DeShannon and Donna Weiss in 1974, and popularized by Kim Carnes in 1981. To say "popularized" may be an understatement – the song held the #1 spot at the *U.S. Billboard Hot 100* chart for nine weeks and stayed in the Top 40 for 20; it helped usher Kim Carnes' album sales up to a staggering eight million copies; and it won for the singer a Grammy Award for Record of the Year.

Its popularity was not just a passing thing, either. It was the third best-seller of the *entire* decade, where that decade – the 1980s – was one of the most important periods of music history. Over the years since its release, the beautiful song found life anew again and again. The Chipmunks gave it a shot in 1982, and Academy Award-winning actress, Gwyneth Paltrow, took it on in 2000 for her film, *Duets*. Pop and dance diva Kylie Minogue added her own spin in 2014, and 10-time Grammy Award winner, Country / Pop crossover star Taylor Swift, enjoyed doing a cover version before massive tour audiences in 2011.

The song, which repeats the line, "*She's got Bette Davis eyes*" over and over, speaks of an irresistible woman of playfulness, self-possession and intrigue – a woman whose "*hands are never cold,*" a woman who can "*make a pro blush,*" a woman who will "*Roll you like you were dice.*"

mother. Treatments at an institution transform her into a more chic and confident woman, who eventually finds forbidden romance with an unhappily married man, Jerry Durrance. By some reports, the songwriters of *Bette Davis Eyes* were drawn in by a particularly compelling scene, where Jerry lights two cigarettes at the same time and hands one to Charlotte. It was the film's signature moment, and a classic cinema moment all on its own.

Bette Davis was 73 years old when the hit song came out, and she reportedly wrote letters to Kim Carnes and the songwriters. In them, she is said to have expressed her appreciation of the song and its role in giving her such a place in modern history, and how she was grateful for how

The imagery is vivid and powerful. Naturally, the songwriters have been asked about what compelled them to write this modern classic. To say the obvious answer, that the actress Bette Davis' titular prying peepers moved them to bring pen to paper, is inadequate; the woman, after all, worked in Hollywood for 50 years and had over 100 film credits to show for it. She started in film in the 1930s, and worked right up to the year of her death in 1989, at age 81. Which of her many incarnations moved them to write one of the greatest pop songs of all time?

Inspiration supposedly came after a viewing of the classic film, *Now, Voyager* (1942). The movie is centered on Charlotte Vale (played by Davis), a privileged but repressed spinster driven towards a nervous breakdown by her overbearing, tyrannical contemporary it made her seem to her grandchildren.

The letters suggest an unexpected, grounded quality in an otherwise proud, confident woman who should never have had any doubt of her permanent position in Hollywood's Parthenon of stars. She was, after all, an accomplished actress with double-digit nominations and two Oscar wins, an Academy Awards record holder for most consecutive acting nominations (alongside Greer Garson), and the first female president of the Academy in 1941 (however short her term had been – for Bette's exits always were as dramatic as her entrances).

She had also become the queen of camp and a beloved icon for the gay community; the subject of many a documentary and biography (including a bestselling, scathing, relationship-ending one by her own daughter); and an off-screen life so fitting to her outsize screen presence that even just a small part of it (her rivalry with fellow screen legend Joan Crawford) is worthy of a hit television series like the recent *Feud* (2017).

She is so striking that her name isn't just on the title of one of the biggest hits of all time – *Bette Davis Eyes* isn't even the first or the last song to mention it. Bette Davis is – just to mention a few - namedropped in iconic, trailblazing superstar Madonna's hit single, *Vogue*; in influential rock band The Kinks' *Celluloid Heroes*; in hit pop-punk band, Good Charlotte's *Silver Screen Romance*; in boy band LFO's *The Girl on TV*; and in Grammy,

Golden Globe, Oscar *and* Nobel Prize-winning artist, Bob Dylan's *Desolation Row*.

When great things are expected from a person, the commonly used phrase is something to the effect of – 'One day, they will write songs about you.' In the case of Bette Davis, she has had more than her fair share of tributes and it is of no surprise; few actors have her ability to captivate and inspire, her courage to challenge, and her willingness to repulse and terrify an audience in the name of her craft. Because here in Hollywood, even if she were in a town of giants, she was an unapologetic titan.

The First Lady of Film

Ruth Elizabeth Davis was born on the 5th of April 1908, to parents Ruth Favor Davis and Harlow Morrell Davis, in Lowell, Massachusetts. When she was around 7 or 8 years old, her parents divorced and her father, a Harvard Law graduate who became a patent lawyer for the government, left their mother to care for Bette and her younger sister, Barbara, all on her own. Ruthie, as Mrs. Davis was known, did everything she could to send Bette and Barbara to a boarding school in New England, reportedly even doing some cleaning work.

Bette attended her mother's alma mater, the Cushing Academy in Massachusetts. She showed an early interest and aptitude for the performing arts. She started with dance, but eventually found the call of theater irresistible. She featured in productions at school and when she graduated, she aimed for the prestigious dramatic schools of New York City.

She was 19 years old, and her first stop was to actress Eva Le Gallienne's Manhattan Civic Repertory in 1927. Not only was she rejected from admittance, she reportedly left having been told that she was "*a frivolous little girl*" with an insincere attitude for the theater! It was quite the verdict, especially as Bette Davis would eventually be known for her on-screen and off-screen theatricality, her joy and devotion for working, and for her courage to take on roles that would have sent any other actresses scurrying away in fear.

A scathing initial rejection was fitting to the Bette Davis narrative, anyway. Her off-screen theatricality was long-established, even before she studied to become an actress. She was born, they say, with a background of lightning and thunder. She had a flair for drama even as a child, when she detested dolls, chopped off her younger sister's beautiful hair, and once reportedly pretended to be blind. She even had a sense of showmanship when it came to her name. She took on the rarer "Bette" as opposed to "Betty" around 1917, based on the suggestion of one of her mother's friends to adopt a change inspired by French author Honoré de Balzac's novel "Cousin Bette." Bette Davis was reportedly convinced that making a small difference in her name can better set her apart.

Her childhood experiences had plenty of fodder for more serious dramatics too, what with her father Harlow and her mother Ruthie's poor relationship. Harlow reportedly did not even want to have Bette, fearing that he and his wife did not have the financial means to become parents at the time Ruthie became pregnant. He even ate separately from his wife and two children, from whom he reportedly had slim reserves of patience. He eventually left them in 1915 and Bette had reportedly always looked upon the divorce a kind of abandonment.

Thus, even at her young age, Bette Davis had a lot of experience and strength to draw from, as well as a devoted and ambitious mother ready to spur her forward. Undeterred by her crushing rejection at the hands of Le Gallienne, Bette managed to secure admission to the John Murray Anderson / Robert Milton School of Theater and Dance, also in New York City. One of her instructors would later describe her as having control and electricity. The storied school counts another legend amongst its alumni – Lucille Ball. She and Bette Davis were classmates there.

Bette Davis paid her theater dues, doing summer stock in Rochester, Upstate New York. But she was quickly crawling her way towards The Great White Way. By 1929, she was in the off-Broadway play, *The Earth Between* at the Provincetown Playhouse in Greenwich Village. It was an important, busy time for the actress. Soon she was also on stage in Ibsen's *The Wild Duck*, and then making her Broadway debut at the age of 21 for *Broken Dishes*. She was an electrifying performer, and would get notice for her debut, as well as for another Broadway appearance, in *Solid South*.

It wasn't long before Hollywood – at the cusp of its Golden Age after the release of talkies, and eager for talents trained in speaking and singing from the theater - came knocking at her door.

Screen Queen Rising

Bette Davis was not a conventional beauty.

She was 5'3", slight, pop-eyed, almost cartoony. She would eventually acquire the nickname, 'little brown wren' in a town of more finely-feathered beauties. Her peers, for example, included Hollywood heavyweights Marlene Dietrich (born 1901), Greta Garbo (born 1905), Joan Crawford (born 1905), Katherine Hepburn (born 1907), and Carole Lombard (born 1908).

When Sam Goldwyn saw her screen test, he was reportedly aghast. But the folks over at Universal Pictures had more vision. By the end of 1930, with less than $100 in their pockets, Bette and her mother, Ruthie (along with their pet terrier), took the leap and headed to Hollywood. She would stay in the entertainment industry for the rest of her life, but no one would have known it on her arrival, or on her initial, forgettable appearances in the movies.

According to Hollywood lore, literally from the time she arrived, she was so unlike the preconceived idea of a movie star that the studio representative assigned to meet her at the train station was not able to find her. At the time, Universal officials who encountered her were unimpressed by her looks and her sex appeal. She got a makeover, but would be tossed into relatively minor roles in unimpressive films. In 1931, she appeared in *Way Back Home* (her debut), as well as *Waterloo Bridge*, *The Bad Sister* and *Seed*.

Her contract wouldn't be renewed and she was getting ready to leave Hollywood and return to the East coast. But her talent was apparent to distinguished Academy Award-winning actor, George Arliss, who at the time was with Warner Brothers and on the lookout for a fine young actress to star with in *The Man Who Played God* (1932). Later, she would say how she initially refused to believe that the famed Mr. Arliss was seeking her out for a role. Thankfully, she took a chance and when she signed on for the role of Grace Blair, Hollywood would never be the same - it was the role that would keep her in town.

The Man Who Played God is based on the play, *The Silent Voice*. It is about a gifted musician deafened during a performance where there was an assassination attempt on his royal audience. The loss of his senses and the consequent decline of his career proved devastating, but with his loyal fiancée by his side, he learned to cope and channel his talents to philanthropic activities. It was made as a silent film featuring Arliss a decade earlier; a practice he'd done before, as when he made a silent and sound film for *Disraeli* (1921 and 1929) and *The Green Goddess* (1923 and 1930).

Mr. Arliss lent gravitas to many a Hollywood picture, and Bette Davis would always credit him for her big break. The distinguished veteran also helped her with technique and character development, and they would work together again for *The Working Man* (1933). The admiration was mutual; he would write about her literally in glowing terms for his 1940 autobiography, describing the 'illuminating flash' and light she could give to words.

Bette signed a multi-year deal with Warner Brothers, and from 1932 to 1934, she made 14 movies, many of them very successful. She would also be known for her powerful performance of complex characters.

It's that gift that would bring her to RKO for *Of Human Bondage* (1934), a role she had pressed studio boss Jack Warner to give her the chance to portray. Warner Bros. loaned her to the rival studio to play the strong-willed, selfish, hateful, vulgar vixen, Mildred Rogers, for a film based on the novel by W. Somerset Maugham. Critics and audiences were enthralled. Bette Davis could play a theoretically unsympathetic character, but still get people on her side. Over the course of her career, her most memorable roles would find her boldly walking that thin, high line – she could be selfish, mean and even villainous, but a leading lady and heroine all the same.

Many young (and even established) actors would have feared such a brand, but Bette Davis could be fearless with her craft. She was unafraid of looking unattractive for the right part. She did not fear being typecast as a villain; she was confident in her own range and besides, as she would later say, they "*…always have the best-written parts.*" And Bette Davis was the best actress to utter them.

Of Human Bondage was a turning point for the actress. Audiences, critics, studios and peers were now paying the rising star rapt attention, and she would be rewarded for her bold performance with her first Academy Award nomination as a write-in nominee.

Bette Davis was not officially nominated for an Academy Award for her performance, and the oversight was received poorly. The cause may have been that she was on loan for *Of Human Bondage*, and so there wasn't much incentive for RKO (which made the film) or Warner (which loaned her out) to promote her performance as Oscar-worthy. There would be claims that Jack Warner may have even campaigned against her, but there is no readily available proof to substantiate this.

Either way, following the scandal over her snub in the Best Actress category, the Academy permitted write-in candidates. It is the first time of only two years that write-in nominations would be allowed. In a way, this is one of the moments that showed how her outsize talent can overwhelm an institution. Bette Davis was the exception rather than the rule.

She lost out to Claudette Colbert of *It Happened One Night,* but she had a very acceptable 'consolation prize' – the accolade put her in a position to command better, more compelling roles. By 1935, she would be walking away with the coveted golden statuette for *Dangerous*.

Rebel Queen of the Screen

Bette Davis top-billed *Dangerous* in the role of struggling actress Joyce Heath, an alcoholic desperate for a comeback. Her redeemer comes in the form of Don Bellows, played by patrician actor, Franchot Tone on loan from MGM (an on loan from his then-fiancée, actress Joan Crawford – but more on this scandal, later). Salvation for the embattled Heath, however, came at the cost of something she was not free to give – marriage. She copes poorly against this dilemma to disastrous results, but finds redemption in paying the consequences of her actions.

It was not considered a stellar script, and Davis had actually been hesitant to take it on. Studio production head Hal Wallis, however, gave her creative heart a boost by his trust that she could make the role special, and added the incentive of engaging two of Warner's top behind-the-scenes talents, Ernest Haller and Orry-Kelly. Haller's (a cameraman) and Kelly's (a costume designer) aesthetic aligned with Davis' brutally realistic vision of an actress in decline.

This is exemplified in the scene when a down-and-out Joyce Heath is found by Don Bellows in a rundown bar. The strong-willed Davis is said to have encountered similarly troubled women when she was in theater, and wanted to convey that gritty realism for her character. The end result was Haller's camera playing it straight, with little regard for flattering angles or lighting. The costume designer, Kelly, on the other hand, dressed the character in simple, aged clothes.

Attention to detail and an electrifying performance by Davis gave the film a winning, grounded vision, and Davis took home the Academy Award for Best Actress in a Leading Role in 1936. The Oscar made her a legitimate star and the reigning "queen" over at Warner Bros.

At a time when studios held so much control over actors though, "Queen" was a relative term. She was referred to as such when her image was sold for a Quaker Puffed Rice advertisement that was printed alongside the line, "*A Breakfast fit for a Queen of the Screen…*" But the award did not really help her progress towards the kinds of material and meaningful roles that she has grown to enjoy and crave – at least, not without her putting up a fight.

In the months following her Oscar win, she was suspended for declining a role. Again, at a time when studios held such power over the industry, actors were expected to toe the line and play whatever was demanded of them - or risk suspension without pay and without the freedom to work anywhere else. Bette Davis took the suspension and headed to Europe hoping to work there, but Warner Bros. was hot on her heels with a contract and the power of the law. She would lose the suit, but return to Hollywood with a louder voice the studio now knew they had to take more seriously. The parts sent her way improved and so did her pay. The trailblazing actress had broken the rules again, only to be rewarded for her efforts.

The Best of Bette

In Bette Davis' extensive filmography, her most important roles include her breakthrough performance with George Arliss in *The Man Who Played God* (1932) – it kept her in Hollywood and gave her another chance at Warner Bros. Then there was *Of Human Bondage* (1934), which had the industry watching and holding their breaths for what she would be able to do next. With *Dangerous* (1935) she had secured her Oscar, and it gave her courage and leverage to buck against the studio system for better roles and better pay. *Now, Voyager* (1942) was so moving it inspired a pop song that brought a then-aging, living legend into modern history. Many other roles would constitute her best work:

- In *The Petrified Forest* (1936), she plays a dreamer diner girl, Gabrielle Maple, who longs for excitement She had Paris in mind, but excitement nevertheless finds her when a dejected writer, Alan Squier (played by Leslie Howard) graces her workplace shortly before the fugitive Duke Mantee (Humphrey Bogart) takes it over. She is off-type here, but still a gifted actress at an intriguing time in her development, as it shows her growing sense of presence and confidence on the screen.

- *Marked Woman* (1937) had her playing Mary Strauber, a hostess at a nightclub who decides to testify against her gangster employer. The consequences of her decision is a brutal beating that leaves her disfigured – a gutsy move on the part of Davis, at a time when beautiful screen imagery was the norm for actresses. Throughout her career, she never feared showing flaw or age or later, even sheer grotesqueness in her face, if she thought it was meaningful to a character. She was unafraid of being perceived as flawed or even ugly as early as the 1930s, but would carry that commitment over to when she shaved her hairline playing Queen Elizabeth I in *The Private Lives of Elizabeth and Essex* (1939) and *The Virgin Queen*

(1955); in *Mrs. Skeffington* (1944) where she showed age, hair-loss and illness; and of course in *Whatever Happened to Baby Jane?* (1962) in her most grotesque, cakey make-up incarnation.

- In *Jezebel* (1938), Bette Davis acted out her Scarlett O'Hara frustrations and blew everyone away as Julie Marston. Davis had wanted badly to play the fiery, irrepressible lead of David O. Selznick's upcoming *Gone with the Wind* (1939), but a deal to loan her out – which included Errol Flynn as Rhett Butler - didn't pan out. *Jezebel* was a fair substitute that shared some of *Gone with the Wind's* attributes – self-absorbed, hard-headed Southern Belle falls in love, loses love, finds personal strength and redemption. *Jezebel* wasn't quite as epic or sweeping, but it is still a classic and it did get five well-deserved Academy Award nominations, including a second Best Actress win for Bette Davis. The role would also get her rave reviews, a cover on *Time* magazine, and a great love affair with acclaimed director, William Wyler.

- Judith Traherne of *Dark Victory* (1939) is said to have been one of Bette Davis' favorite parts, for it allowed her to display the range of her considerable talents. She starts as a radiant, carefree socialite whose world turns upside down when diagnosed with an inoperable brain tumor. She decides to live her life fully, to pursue happiness, to give and take love… but is always shadowed by what's to come. It was a tour de force worthy of another Oscar nomination – except that year, the award would be brought home by Vivien Leigh, the stunning and talented actress who secured the role of Scarlett O'Hara in *Gone with the Wind*. Fans of Bette Davis can't help but wonder at what Bette Davis could have done with the irresistible Scarlett if she had only been given the chance.

- After the success of *Jezebel*, Wyler and Davis made film magic anew in the film noir classic, *The Letter* (1940). Bette plays Leslie Crosby, adulterous wife to the administrator of a rubber plantation. It opens with a merciless Leslie pumping bullets on her lover and later claiming self-defense – an excuse threatened by a letter that could expose her lies.

Theoretically, Leslie isn't a sympathetic character, but Davis is captivating in how she infuses the character with complexity. She was just as compelling in her last collaboration with Wyler, for *The Little Foxes* in 1941. In it, she plays the selfish Regina, who was not above using her own family for her nefarious purposes. In one key scene, she coldly watches her dying husband trying to crawl up a flight of stairs for his medicines. She was chilling and irresistible to watch.

Throughout her career, Bette Davis held such passion for her work. According to her, beyond life's disappointments, work is that one thing which *"really stands by a human being."* She would also be quoted for statements like *"it is only work that truly satisfies"* or that she felt a profound, sweet joy *"at the end of a good day's work."* In her later years when she fell gravely ill, she was open about the sheer *"terror"* at the prospect of never being able to work again, when it was that one thing that she *"always very much loved."*

That value she placed on her profession was reflected in her constant drive to keep performing. In one interview, she had claimed that one of the things she feared was a fate like that of a faded star who needed to auction off her things, and so she did not like owning things that couldn't fit in a trunk. And so, on and on she worked, almost right up until the end of her life.

Her two Oscars and string of hits had made her the Queen over at Warners when she was just in her early 30 years of age, but even good things must come to an end. Critical and commercial disappointments during the 1940s, including *Deception* (1946) which had reportedly lost money, ultimately led to her studio releasing her in 1949 after 19 years of keeping her under contract. Bette wouldn't be down for very long, though, and soon, she would be wowing the town again in Mankiewicz's *All About Eve* (1950):

- Bette Davis got 10 Best Actress Oscar nominations in her life, but Joseph L. Mankiewicz's *All About Eve*, for which she was of course nominated, is probably where she played her most memorable

role and uttered her most iconic line –
"*Fasten your seatbelts. It's going to be a*
bumpy night." The part of Margo
Channing actually wasn't meant for her –
she was a replacement for Claudette
Colbert, who had been injured. But the
character Margo, a theater star under
threat from an interloping former fan
overly eager to take over her personal
and professional life, was characterized
by Davis so indelibly that it is now
difficult to imagine the role being played
by anyone else.

Bette Davis' career had a brief resurgence
after she brought the unforgettable Margo
Channing to the screen, and she played the
lead in *The Star* (1952). In this movie, Davis

plays a down-and-out, award-winning actress, Margaret Elliott, whose star has faded. She was no longer working in film and she has become mired in legal and financial troubles. She has a chance at love and a new life, but still struggles to reclaim the glories of her old one. The film was supposedly about Bette Davis' Hollywood rival, Joan Crawford… which was reportedly one of the reasons why it had been appealing to Bette Davis!

The First Lady of Film again found herself in the Oscar race for Best Actress, but the movie did not perform to expectations at the box office. Bette Davis would then appear in few other major screen projects throughout the fifties. But Bette was a true artist with a work ethic to match, and she found other outlets for her gift and love of performance. She diversified the media where she shared her talent. After finishing her work on *The Star*, she headed back to Broadway for *Two's Company*, which opened in December, 1952 and closed in March, 1953 after just 90 performances; it received poor critical reception. She also lent her talents to television. While some of her peers had been skeptical of the medium, Bette was an early adapter and made numerous appearances in several TV series throughout the decade.

It was a light ten years compared to her previous outputs, and it was during this era in her life that she actually found time to be a wife and a mother. Earlier in the decade, she became romantically involved with and eventually married her *All About Eve* co-star, Gary Merrill. For a few of her work's quiet years, she could devote herself to family.

Unfortunately, she later claimed it was when Gary fell out of love for her. The couple went on tour performing on *The World of Carl Sandburg*, but their marriage was already on shaky ground. In 1960 they divorced, and the play made its way to Broadway without Merrill. It opened in September, 1960 and closed in October, 1960 after only 29 performances. She eventually had a longer running show, with Tennessee Williams' *The Night of the Iguana*, which opened in December, 1961. But the real monster hit of the decade for Davis was the movie, *What Ever Happened to Baby Jane*?

- Director Robert Aldrich's *Whatever Happened to Baby Jane?* (1962) brought storied rivals, Bette Davis and Joan

Crawford together on screen for their *only* film together. The psychological thriller has Davis playing Jane, a former child star ruined by a lost career, drink, and worsening mental illness. Crawford plays Jane's older sister Blanche, a wheelchair-bound former Hollywood actress. The sisters have a claustrophobic, co-dependent relationship, with an immobile Blanche completely reliant on Jane, while Jane is financially at the mercy of Blanche, burdened by her care, and tortured by her own demons. They are so hopelessly tied together, even as their bonds run with long-standing resentment and jealousy. As Jane descends further into madness, she cruelly drags her sister down with her in increasingly sadistic acts gradually escalating to the point of murder. Bette

Davis is horrifying and so intentionally grotesque in this piece of Hollywood gothic, and her turn as Jane got her yet another Academy Award nomination, the last of her life. The campy spectacle was a big hit, which gave a boost to the two actress's flailing careers.

And so, with a big hit in her hands, Bette Davis was able to continue with her beloved work. She took on leads and she took on character roles. She performed in a variety of genres, but found a particular home in melodramas and thrillers. At one point, she had even donned an eye patch for *The Anniversary* (1968). She appeared in both movies and in television. She would even pick up an Emmy in 1979 as Outstanding

Lead Actress in a Limited Series or a Special, for *Strangers: The Story of a Mother and Daughter*.

She really came to embrace the medium of television. Television embraced her back. The peak of her popularity may have been in Hollywood's Golden Age from the 1930s to the early 1950s, but Bette Davis was a frequent presence on small screens all over the country, via made-for-TV movies, TV shows, and repeat showings of her classic films. In this way, she had become a star across media and a star across generations.

It wasn't always easy for Bette Davis, though. She always had to fight for her place in the limelight. She was an intelligent woman with self-awareness about this too. Later in life, she conceded that she had on occasion been rude, insufferable and uncompromising… because she *"had no time for pleasantries."*

When she first came to Hollywood, she fought to get a contract. She fought to stay employed. Once employed, she fought for more creative control and better pay. When she reached the top, she fought to stay there. As her stature waned, she fought for parts. As her health declined, she fought against her own body to continue working.

After she died, she was buried in Los Angeles with a tombstone that reads, *"She did it the hard way."* But she had to; she was tough and she was a fighter, and she bucked and kicked with everything she had. She used her talents, she used her smarts, she used that unassailable, quick-wit, and she fought with ballsy nerve.

In the 1960s, for example, after filming wrapped on *What Ever Happened to Baby Jane?* but before it came out as a massive hit, she may have worried for what the future held for her… enough that she had taken out a newspaper ad for her services! Among the choice lines was, "*…Mobile still and more affable than rumor would have it. Wants steady employment in Hollywood…*"

It was classic Bette Davis; whip-smart and biting, with dark humor and a dash of commentary. Hollywood observers note that she probably wasn't in such desperate straits to need an ad like this, but in a way it was a critique of an industry that was taking her talent and years of service for granted, and of how there were such limited opportunities available for older women in Hollywood.

And then, *What Ever Happened to Baby Jane* came out to punctuate her point. There was still a place for a performer of her caliber in entertainment. What she did not know at the time, is that there would *always* be a place for her in entertainment.

She was also aware however, that her devotion to work came at the cost of other things – most painfully, her failed romances and troubled family life.

'The Lonely Life…'

Just as the historical Queen Elizabeth I was married to England (a character she would portray on film twice), Bette Davis, Queen of Hollywood, was "The First Lady of Film." She was a woman married to the movies. Work seemed to be her only lasting partner, for she would have trouble being a "first lady" to anyone else.

Bette Davis, according to some Hollywood commentators, may have been handicapped by her harsh experiences with her distant, disapproving father. It had a negative impact on her relationships, but then again, so could have many other factors, including how focused she was on her career; how little time she could devote to her relationships; and how her men were able to cope with her fierce personality, hectic lifestyle, the spotlight on their life, and her greater success compared to their own.

For Bette Davis, work always seemed to come first, but she was also a woman who liked men, had confessed to an appetite for sex, and craved companionship. Sometimes, her professional and personal needs just couldn't complement each other, resulting in a string of husbands and broken relationships.

"Ham" (married: 1932-1938)

Bette first found love with Harmon Oscar Nelson Jr. – the "Ham" (as she called him) to her "Spuds" (as he called her). They were together during their time at Cushing Academy, and they married at Yuma in 1932. He was a moderately successful musician and bandleader, and he and Bette would have long spells apart when he toured with an orchestra and when she was immersed in the demands of her own work.

When they divorced, he claimed that she neglected him in pursuit of her career. The end of their six-year marriage, however, would be plagued by harsher tales too. It couldn't have been easy if he was, as has been reported, lampooned for allegedly earning a tenth of what she was making. There were also allegations of physical abuse, and claims of multiple abortions done at his behest so as not to disrupt the trajectory of her career and the momentum of her success. Then there were also reports of Bette's affair with notorious moneyman Howard Hughes...

Howard Hughes

The Hollywood power player, multi-millionaire lothario was linked to a bevy of greats, among them Ava Gardner, Olivia de Havilland and Rita Hayworth… but he reportedly told Bette Davis (whether sincerely or as a gimmick), that she was the only one who could help him climax. It had the desired effect, and he landed another legendary conquest. But the ever-witty dame harbored no illusions about the claim and had been quoted as saying, "*it was cheaper than buying gifts.*"

According to one account, he and Bette had their dalliances when her husband Ham was away. When Ham found out, he allegedly had the erring pair monitored by a private eye, documented their affair, and threatened to make it publicly known. There were wild tales of a hit placed and retracted on Ham, and of big pay-offs in exchange for destroyed recordings. Divorce and leaving the marriage with a considerable share of his wife's assets, seems almost sedate compared to lore like this.

Around the time that all the drama was unfolding, Bette was also busy working on *Jezebel*, and ensnaring another major Hollywood figure – the director, William Wyler.

William Wyler – The One That Got Away

Newly-divorced, Hollywood director William Wyler first came into Bette Davis' life when he helmed *Jezebel*. Wyler was an artist and perfectionist, whose insistence on take after take after take would bring the picture behind schedule and over budget, but to stunning results. He was a strong personality with vision, and Bette not only stood up for him when the studio executives became dissatisfied by his performance, she also gave him her professional commitment… as well as her heart.

Not right away, of course, and not easily (this was, after all, Bette Davis). They had extended battles of wills on set, and she would repeatedly counter whatever direction he gave her before following. They found each other brilliant and irresistible. Eventually, under Wyler's direction, she was able to refine her techniques and churn out some of the greatest work of her life, as was the case in *Jezebel,* and later in *The Letter* (1940) and *The Little Foxes* (1941).

They had a passionate affair that is said to have resulted in a pregnancy that Bette felt compelled to abort, so as not to force William into a tenuous position. He reportedly asked her to marry him at one point, but she demurred and played hard to get, which she would come to regret later when he ended up marrying someone else. She always considered him the great love of her life, though Wyler wouldn't be as effusive; he found her too intense and emotional.

Arthur Farnsworth (married: 1940-1943)

Arthur Farnsworth has been described as a former commercial airline pilot, aircraft engineer and innkeeper. Most people, however, would know him best as the second husband of Bette Davis, most distinguishable amongst the lineup for his mysterious death.

Farnsworth and Davis knew each other in high school, and when they married in 1940, it was a surprise to most. They were together up until he died amid strange circumstances in 1943, and the actress was reportedly in such a hysterical state over the tragedy that she had to be placed under the care of a physician.

The circumstances around his passing remain clouded by questions. Farnsworth was reportedly found unconscious along Hollywood Boulevard and would pass away a few days later. He had apparently collapsed, and an autopsy would later reveal that the sidewalk fall came as a result of dizziness induced by pressure from a blood clot in his head. The blood clot was the result of a skull injury taken before the final fall.

Bette Davis was interrogated as a routine part of the ensuing investigation, and she revealed that her husband had taken a stair fall weeks earlier, while running to answer the phone. That injury was considered the cause of the clot. In a later theory, it has been suggested that Farnsworth may have been struck behind the head after he was discovered with his attacker's wife. Either way – Arthur Farnsworth died at the young age of 35, from the complications and belated effects of a head injury.

William Grant Sherry (married: 1945 – 1950)

Bette Davis next found love after World War II, in muscular ex-Marine, William Grant

Sherry. Sherry has been described as an artist, landscape artist, and masseur. When they met, he reportedly did not know who she was!

Troubles for the couple reportedly started early; he allegedly threw a trunk at her during their honeymoon. It wouldn't be the only thing he would throw at Bette; an ice bucket was said to be amongst the projectiles lobbed the actress' way.

Davis and Sherry had a child a few years after their wedding, Barbara Davis "B.D." Sherry, when Bette was 39. A child, however, couldn't save the marriage. Relations did not improve between husband and wife, and the couple divorced after five years together. The parting was, again, not without controversy; Mr. Sherry ended up marrying B.D.'s nanny, Marion Richards.

This difficult period in Bette's life also coincided with troubles in her career. A series of disappointing releases ended Bette's 19-year stint at Warners in 1949.

Gary Merrill (married 1950-1960)

For Bette, the new stage in her career led to a new stage in her love life too.

Bette Davis worked with actor Gary Merrill in the hit, *All About Eve*. They married just a few weeks after her divorce with William Grant Sherry was finalized in mid-1950. They adopted a baby girl shortly afterwards and named her Margot Mosher Merrill. The couple later adopted another child, whom they named Michael.

Merrill and Davis remained with each other for a while. He was the last of her husbands, and they stayed together for the longest time, from 1950 to 1960. Because her career was winding down in the 1950s, she also got to play a more domestic role in her marriage. They even lived in a farm in Maine with B.D. and their two kids.

Unfortunately for Bette, her domestic life still didn't work out. Their first adopted child was diagnosed with developmental issues and had to be sent away for care in a handicapped home. Gary's macho streak couldn't have been too helpful either; he was said to be a mean drunk who was rude to guests and willing to batter his wife.

It may seem uncharacteristic how the fiery Davis tolerated such treatment for so long, until we get a better idea of the larger battle she may have been fighting at the time; she wasn't just sticking around for the love of Gary. By some accounts, she was looking at this last marriage as a final chance at love, and an indicator of whether or not she could be a wife. By 1960 she conceded failure and they parted ways.

Later in life though, she came to realize that her failed efforts at being a wife were not wholly her fault. Of Gary and her husbands, she would say that no one seemed *"man enough to become Mr. Bette Davis…"*

Looking back at all the accomplishments of her life and long career – she was probably right!

Franchot Tone: The Birth of a Feud

In some ways, one of the longest relationships Bette Davis was able to keep was with fellow Hollywood legend, Joan Crawford. Unfortunately, it was more a feud than a friendship, and would last longer than whatever she had with most of the men who had come into her colorful life.

Surprisingly, Bette and Joan had a lot in common; they were both tough, pragmatic, modern and sensual. They had a string of love affairs and marriages, and notoriously troubled relationships with their children. But at one point in their lives, they shared something that precluded them from ever being friendly – an interest in actor, Franchot Tone, an MGM player famous for the hit, *Mutiny on the Bounty* (1935).

He was Bette Davis' leading man in *Dangerous*, and she is said to have fallen for the well-brought-up, Cornell-educated, New Yorker. Her marriage with Ham was not doing well at the time and she ended up having a big crush on her co-star. Later, she would say that while she had a personal and professional admiration for Tone, it was unrequited (this would be contested by allegations that the two actually did have an affair). She would even be reported as confessing to jealously watching as he and Joan Crawford, with whom he was engaged at the time, met daily for lunch. Tone and Crawford married in 1935 shortly after the filming wrapped, but divorced after four years.

Whether or not he and Bette actually had a fling or something more than a fling is unknown, especially as there would be conflicting accounts even from Bette herself. Decades after Davis and Tone starred together in 1935, her story changed. The shift has been attributed to either honesty from old age or illness, or an illusion, or an act. Either way, she reportedly claimed in 1987 that she would never forgive Crawford for ruthlessly taking Tone away from her.

Whatever it was that they had (if they had anything at all), the Davis-Tone link ended quickly, and would be long outlived by the legendary feud it allegedly sparked. The two women would have multiple run-in's in a town that gradually became too small for two screen queens.

Davis reportedly disliked Crawford and alleged that Crawford used sex to move forward in her career. During the Oscars ceremony when Bette won the Best Actress nod for *Dangerous*, for example, she reportedly did not expect to win and did not even want to go, so she arrived in a simple dress for the affair. After she won, Tone embraced her warmly, but had to prompt his new wife, Joan Crawford, to attention. Crawford, resplendent in her high formals, reportedly dryly commented on Bette's *"lovely frock."*

When Bette Davis' Hollywood fortunes started to diminish in the mid to late 1940s, Crawford (formerly of MGM) moved in on Davis' Warner Bros. territory; she secured the dressing room next to Bette's. By some reports it was not an altogether antagonistic move, and Crawford was said to have tried to initiate a truce with gifts and flowers.

Bette didn't bite though, and when one of Crawford's first major efforts for her new home, *Mildred Pierce* (1945), won her an Oscar and a lucrative contract, it didn't please the beleaguered Warners queen either. It probably did not help that the role was one Bette had allegedly turned down!

The heated rivalry between Bette Davis and Joan Crawford became part of Hollywood lore. Sometimes they perpetuated it by their comments against each other, and other times they doused it in saccharine denial. There was also a surprising twist to this tale. If true, Crawford, who is said to have indulged her sensuality with both men and women, might have actually felt an attraction or curiosity for Bette Davis.

The decades' old tension – whether it stemmed from a man, sexual attraction, or professional rivalry - boiled over when the two women were cast to play dysfunctional sisters in the psychological thriller, *What Ever Happened to Baby Jane*?

The partnership was reportedly suggested by Joan Crawford, who had past history working with the director, Robert Aldrich in *Autumn Leaves* (1956). It was theoretically a marketable - if gimmicky – proposition, to cast the rivals in the perfect vehicle to bring their tension to the screen. Nothing about it was easy, though; from the sourcing of project backers to negotiating between the two divas, to dealing with their on-set tension and sometimes, outright antagonism.

It was hard to manage two women wrapped up in deep, long-standing, mutual dislike of each other, but at that point of their lives they were again rather similar - they were two gifted but aging actresses fighting to keep their place in Hollywood. The project pushed through, but in the tight quarters and constant company of a set, they had plenty of occasions to needle each other. Among the choice encounters?

A scene that called for fake physical violence apparently ended up with a real kick from Bette Davis' shoe to Crawford's head. Crawford retaliated by wearing weights for a scene where Bette's character had to drag her around; Davis hurt her back doing the heavy lifting.

When it came out, the bizarre movie was a hit. Davis and Crawford not only made a killing, they made a comeback and forged yet another place for themselves in Hollywood history. They were legends apart, yes, but they were legends anew together.

Not that the film's success did anything to mend fences. Davis was nominated for a Best Actress award at the Oscars and Crawford was not; but Crawford had arranged to accept the Oscar for another nominee, Anne Bancroft. When Bancroft triumphed over Davis, it was Crawford holding the statuette that had escaped her. Crawford had also been accused of campaigning against her co-star.

Bette Davis' next major film, *Hush, Hush, Sweet Charlotte* (1964) with the same director, Robert Aldrich, was originally meant to reunite the rivals. However, Crawford eventually bowed out due to illness… if she was really gravely ill or not is uncertain, but it certainly couldn't have been encouraging when Davis allegedly arranged for the cast and crew to pose for a photograph with Coca-Cola – the chief competition of Pepsi Co., the company run by Crawford's late husband, Alfred Steele, and where she had been a spokesperson and board member. It wasn't the first time Bette Davis allegedly used soda to needle Crawford; if Hollywood lore is to be believed, she's once asked for a Coke machine in her dressing room on the set of *What Ever Happened to Baby Jane*, too.

At the time of this writing, it's been decades since both women's deaths – Crawford passed away in 1977 and Bette died in 1989 - but their storied rivalry only added to their individual magnetism. The strife between the two women would be reintroduced to contemporary audiences via the Ryan Murphy-helmed hit television series, *Feud* (2017).

Thus, as surely as *Bette Davis Eyes* brought Davis into the 1980s, a new generation met her acquaintance yet again.

Bette Davis as a Mother

The two women had several similarities, but the most glaring one was probably their difficult relationships with their children.

When Joan Crawford died, she had disinherited her adopted children, Christina and Christopher. About a year afterwards, Christina released the savage tell-all, *Mommie Dearest*, depicting Joan as an abusive, sadistic, drunk. The shocking revelations included Crawford's severe aversion to wire hangers and beating her child with one; other instances of physical abuse; starvation as punishment; and getting tied up in bed.

Whether completely factual or not – for a number of accounts would later contest some of the claims – *Mommie Dearest* made for truly compelling reading and was so cinematic it yielded a Faye Dunaway starrer, a film of the same name in 1981. Shelves would also be stocked with updated editions on its 20th and 30th-year anniversaries, showing continuing relevance for years to come.

Bette Davis was still very much alive and active in the industry when the book about her great rival came out. She has been quoted as saying Crawford did not deserve such a detestable act from someone she had saved from being an orphan. She went on to say that she felt sorry for Crawford, but understood that her rival wouldn't want her of all people to feel pity. She then said the pain would be "*Unimaginable*" if her daughter, B.D., submitted her to the same situation…

… and indeed, she wouldn't have had to imagine it at all.

In 1985, B.D. Hyman published *My Mother's Keeper* about her own difficulties with her mom, Bette. It was poorly received, what with Bette still alive and in frail health. Bette

Davis had previously suffered a broken hip, a mastectomy and a stroke, so Hyman's timing was regarded as somewhat cruel. B.D., however, would claim purer motivations; she said she had been trying to reach out to her mother but was ignored, so she brought her issues before the public so that Davis may finally acknowledge them. Whatever her motivations were, her revelations were rough too.

Bette was depicted as a heavy drinker, who referred to her handicapped child, Margot, as "*retarded*." She was shown as a mentally cruel, overly possessive egomaniac, and an embittered man-hater who discouraged ties between B.D. and her father, William Grant Sherry. There were even claims of how Bette had tried to sabotage the relationship between B.D. and the man who would be her husband.

The backlash was severe, and B.D. would get it even from familial quarters. Her adoptive brother, Michael Merrill, cut ties with her. Bette cut B.D. and her children, Ashley and Justin Hyman, from her will, too. And it was very unfortunate, considering Bette had harbored such hopes for B.D. and after her, her grandson Ashley as well. When he was 11 years old, she helped him get cast in a project with her. Reports indicate she treated her grandson as a professional, and was pleased by his potential, just as she had been pleased by B.D. when the young girl played a bit part in *What Ever Happened to Baby Jane*?

The relationship between Bette and her biological daughter was fairly complicated.

B.D. had claimed a loving childhood, but had some qualms about Bette's part in her adult life. Much of their grief may be traced to 1963, when Bette and B.D. were in Cannes to promote *What Ever Happened to Baby Jane*, which of course starred Davis but as earlier mentioned, also featured a teenaged B.D. in a small role. There, the young girl met Jeremy Hyman, who she would marry just a year later. She was 16 and he was twice her age.

Whatever the cause for the tome, *My Mother's Keeper* pained the actress greatly, and mother and daughter severed ties. Davis eventually took the time to finish her own bestselling autobiography, *This 'n That* (1987), part of which was written while she recovered from a stroke. Though the book detailed her battle with illness, it also contained an open letter addressed to her daughter, including the lines, *"I've been your keeper all these many years…,"* a clever hit, of course, on the title of B.D.'s controversial book.

This 'n That was actually Bette Davis' second biography. She had previously penned *A Lonely Life* in 1962. In it, she mentioned how human relationships were not dependable, and that it was in work where one could find true satisfaction. She would affirm that statement later, describing work as *"the least disappointing relationship"* one could have. In her history, save perhaps for her son, Michael (who defended her and later established a foundation in her name), many of her relationships did indeed end up disappointing her. But her work – her work was as enriching for her as it was for the world of entertainment.

Legacy: Larger Than Life

Bette Davis had a very singular approach to her craft. To be natural, she said, was not the point of acting and so she never bothered with being low-key. Acting, she is reported as saying, "*should be larger than life.*" But it wasn't only her performances that were massive; she herself loomed large over everyone else. She harbored no illusions or pretensions that she was anything other than an outsize personality. She was aware of her talents and what these talents entitled her to, but she also imbued her gifts with a sense of responsibility. Of her reputation as being exacting and difficult at work, she had once said that she had to have a care for her output because "*It's your name up there.*"

Providing quality work was also about accountability.

She was fearless and relentless, a true trailblazer who was aware of her own worth, and made sure everyone else knew about it too. In one endearing story, part of the Kennedy Center Honors' practice was to send out letters to people distinguished in their fields, asking them for suggestions on honorees for the year. In the early 1980s, Bette sent her suggestion to Washington: "*Me.*"

A few years later, the 79-year-old would indeed be honored by the Kennedy Center in 1987, in a ceremony at the White House of President Ronald Reagan – whom she had actually starred with in *Dark Victory*.

She played it cool of course, but it must have been gratifying to thus be honored by an industry she had paid so much to continue to be a part of. Bette Davis loved awards and didn't take the accolades sent her way for granted. Of her Oscars, she once said she was never "*a bit modest about them*." She had also been quoted as admitting to a sense of 'greediness' about them, in that though she had "*gotten just about every award there is,*" she just "*can't have too many.*"

Bette Davis was prone to hyperbole, but when she mentioned getting pretty much all the awards out there, she wasn't too far off the mark. Aside from Oscars, an Emmy, and the Kennedy Center honor earlier mentioned, she was given the American Film Institute's Life Achievement Award in 1977 – the first woman to receive the distinction.

Much of her later awards were, appropriately, not just about individual film work anymore, but the body of her contributions. In 1989, she was also celebrated at the yearly Tribute of the Film Society of Lincoln Center. There were 2,700 people in the audience, and they gave her an almost 2-minute standing ovation. Her response? An iconic line from *Beyond the Forest* (1949): *"What a dump!"*

What a legend.

In 1980, she was also awarded the Defense Department's Distinguished Civilian Service Medal, for her work with the Hollywood Canteen during World War II. Here, she found a way to merge her dedication to her craft with her patriotism. When the United States went to war after the attack on Pearl

Harbor, thousands of Hollywood on and off-screen players responded to the call to serve. Davis couldn't fight in the field, but she did what she could at home by helping to establish and run a club catering to uniformed American recruits and Allies. She, along with actor John Garfield and businessman Jules Stein, were the force behind The Hollywood Canteen. It was a refuge of food and entertainment for uniformed men. Thousands of Hollywood workers – including actors and actresses! – volunteered at the Canteen to serve those who served the country. On some evenings, men about to go on dangerous tours even got to dance with a celebrity. There were lesser starlets helping out of course, but if the tales are accurate, Marlene Dietrich and Hedy Lamarr had washed dishes here. Rita

Hayworth served food. Betty Grable was there to welcome the millionth guest to walk in too – with a kiss. The project was a big success, and inspired the movie, *Hollywood Canteen* (1944). Over the years that it was open, estimates are that it welcomed 3 million servicemen to its doors.

These achievements are lofty and she had every right to be proud of them, for they cost her a lot too. She had paid for her achievements with a mostly lonely personal life, as well as exhausting effort as her health declined.

In 1983, she was diagnosed with breast cancer and needed a mastectomy. Shortly afterwards, she suffered a stroke. Months later, she had to have surgery for a broken hip. Her hurts would have a dire impact on her appearance and mobility, but she moved onwards as she does, always onwards with working. Through the difficulties of illness and old age, she fought on and continued to appear on film and television. She even continued to work after her daughter B.D.'s scathing book came out.

Through the vicissitudes of life she always had her beloved work and the industry was lucky to still have her, but by the late-1980s, they – *we* - wouldn't have her for very long anymore.

Her last major part was in *The Whales of August* (1987), where she played Libby Strong, a cantankerous, blind widow staying in her family's summer cottage with her sister, played by fellow Hollywood gem, Lillian Gish. They both gave powerhouse performances in roles that were a gift to accomplished actresses at the twilight of their years and careers.

Her last actual film, however, was *Wicked Stepmother* (1989), which she left mid-production; the first she would abandon thus in her career. She was initially said to have left for health reasons. She needed extensive dental work and suffered severe weight loss from its effects. But eventually, Bette Davis aired out her grievances against the director's style and wanted to distance herself from the project. It was rewritten and the final cut still included her, and so though the world was gifted with a final Bette Davis movie, it wasn't her best one.

Not that anything could have been so horrible as to dent her legacy at that point of her life. More than a slander on her work ethic, her exit from *Wicked Stepmother* showed she was, at 81, ailing but apparently still feisty. But she had also suffered a series of strokes, and her cancer would return. When the doctors informed her the cancer had spread and her situation was terminal, she was told to just go on about her life.

In Bette's case, "life" was work and so, work she did.

In 1989, she was dying of cancer, in pain and had impaired mobility. But there was an award with her name on it at a film festival in San Sebastian, Spain, and so she had to get it. From Los Angeles she headed off to Europe, but she wouldn't make it back home alive.

In the French leg of her return to the United States, she became too weak and needed to be hospitalized. She died a few days later, on the 6th of October. Shortly before she died, she was still busy updating her 1962 autobiography, *The Lonely Life*, and catching it up with what transpired in her life since it first came out.

All-too-fittingly, just as she closed her life with that award in Spain, the last of the five new chapters she prepared for the book was written in San Sebastian. The last chapter in her life, and the last chapter of her book… It's almost, well, cinematic.

No one could have written her own life out better than Bette.

Printed in Great Britain
by Amazon